Tangled Thoughts

Staci Guenther

BookLeaf
Publishing

Presentation by *BookLeaf Publishing*

Web: www.bookleafpub.com

E-mail: info@bookleafpub.com

ISBN: 9789357214582

First edition 2023

To John for always believing in me.

ACKNOWLEDGEMENT

Thank you to my husband John and my children Coty, Philip, and Savannah.

PREFACE

Poetry has always been a path for me to experience and share my view of the world around me. Poems are a way to express emotions and tell other people a new way to look at a situation or activity. Connection between people is what life is all about.

Music

Music seems to fill the air
Everywhere I go,
There is music in falling rain
Falling leaves and winter snow.
If you listen carefully
You can hear it too,
Music comes from in the heart
And turns a dull sky blue.

Why?

Why does love come and go
Faster than the falling snow?
The pain seems to last forever
But forget about it and it will leave,
So you think.
Maybe you are wrong
Then what will you do?
Will you suffer years
Because of the untrue?
Or will you conquer
Emotion, Hurt, Hatred
and survive?
Pick the ending or the beginning
Why?
Because love is an illusion,
A trip to the unknown
A door to the end.
Pick your fate
To love or not
The flow of emotions
Will someday end,
Especially for you
My friend.

The Fairy

A girl was coloring
One spring day
And I asked her
To come and play
Among the rocks at the edge
Of the brook that was there.
She said she's come
And it seemed
She had walked upon the air.
She said her name was Mary
And she belonged to the family
Whose mother had died
In the glen by the dairy.
I felt sorry for her
And wished her good luck
With the snap of a finger
She was gone.

Decide

What happens when you can't decide
Between those that you love,
Indecision won't subside
It soars around like a dove.

The things not found in one person
Can be found in another,
But perhaps no one can
Replace you very first lover.

Troubles just like this one
Are hard to overcome,
While you think, have some fun
And soon it will be done.

Take some time
Follow your heart,
All the true signs
That's where they start.

Untouchable

Wanton, intense desire
Happens when I think of you.
When you are on my mind
I hope for dreams to come true.

You will never know my feelings,
I hold back so you won't see,
I don't think you would be happy
With someone who is like me.

Maybe I simply doubt myself
And would be right for you,
Getting out of my own way
Is what I should do.

People do not see themselves
As other people may
This is what makes us untouchable
Keeping people away.

It is much easier to find the faults
Then see our own wonderful gifts,
Allowing others to help us find them
Stops kindness from being adrift.

The Wanderer

6

The days were short
Upon the lake
As I sat to watch
Wide awake.
The birds were chirping
Ready to go
Before the fall
Of winter's snow.
As I sat there
All alone
I realized,
There's no place like home.

Loneliness

An old woman sat with her little dog
One evening in late summer
The woman did this every night
Late into the fall.
All her neighbors thought of her
As someone strange and laughed
When she would ask
"Please let me be."
They never left the woman alone
Nor did they offer company,
They asked her why she sat there
With just her little dog,
The answer that she gave them was,
"he's all I've got in this life,
This dog has all my love,
But you folks don't understand,
You think I'm just a quack.
But hear me now and listen well,
I know just where it's at."
Then she turned around and walked away
Into her little house,
They never bothered her again,
Because she killed herself.

The Piccolo

8

The sound was high,
The sound was shrill,
It was heard through
Valley and hill,
It was heard up high
And way down low
The sound that was heard
Was the piccolo.

Everything

9

Everything within this world
Has a place to be,
Whether it is in the sky
Or way out in the sea.

Everything has a need
To have love, comfort, and care
If underneath the water
Or floating in the air.

There is a need for everything
In one way or another,
No matter what that something is
Object, animal, or brother.

Silence

Dreaded Silence
Overtaking us
Ruling our lives.

Overwhelming Noise
Killing the silence
Taking its time.

When Silence returns
Quiet time
Quickened pace.

The Noise
Slowing us down
Losing the race.

Goodbyes

There's always something
We have to say goodbye to,
No matter how much it hurts
It is necessary to do.
We have to learn to let go
To move on to more,
Sometimes saying goodbye
Is the key to the next door.
When you have to say it
Try your hardest to forget,
Whatever you have said goodbye to
Will take time to get over it.
Find a friend in the new phase
Someone to help you through,
Talk about what you have lost
To gain something anew.

Waterfall Dreams

12

Waterfall dreams
Sparkle with lives
And nature's beauty.
Pictured in the glorious falls
Are faces forming haunting reminders
Of memories and sweethearts.
The faces of those you love
Will never leave your soul,
The beauty can be personal
Or shared with another,
You may see your childhood,
They could see a beautiful girl,
But together the images can create
Harmony in the world.

Night Upon the Shore

The sun set as I walked along
The beach was golden sand,
The waved cascaded onto the place
Created for immortal man.
I felt like flying over the waves
On that starry night,
When all of nature came to me
And blessed me with the sight.
Nature is enduring
Lasting forevermore
I became wiser and more aware
That night upon the shore.

No Explaining

There is no explaining
The way you make me feel,
When I am around you
I fall head over heels.
I love what you do to do
The way you make me smile,
Just for that moment in time
I'd go the extra mile.
I love to have you near me
I wish it always true,
All my thoughts by day and night
Are just of me and you.

Mystery

15

Life is a bubble
Filled with mystery,
If you solved them
Admired you would be.
How often do you wonder
What life is all about?
Do you ponder until you find
A way to ease your doubts?
Find the ways to discover
Exactly what it would mean
To live life to the fullest
Fulfilling all your dreams.
The mystery is distinctive
Each has their own to solve,
The answer is in your journey
The ending then resolved.

Feelings

Confusion sets in
As I try to see
All of the feelings
Settled in me.
I want to love,
To like, to hate
The challenge is
To mediate
Between these things
To figure out
What should be done
Besides sit and pout.
I want to be able
To settle my life
Without frustration,
Sadness, or strife.
What should I do?
What should I say?
Help me to see
What to do today.

Sunset

17

The colors flow into sunset
As waves strike upon the shore,
When I dream about seeing it
I want it more and more.
I want to watch the horizon
Burst into colors on a beach
With my one and only love
Sitting within my reach.

Runaway

Far from home
A young girl sat
In a bus station
When she saw a rat
She screamed for help
But no one came
No one wanted to touch her
Or learn her name.
The poor little runaway
Now, all by herself
All alone on a hard bench
Trying to sleep, needing help.
She's tired and lonely
She can't find her way back
But no one will help her,
Help her find the path
Home to her papa and mama
Home where she should go,
How she will ever get there
The little girl does not know.

No Love

Sometimes I wish there was no love
Upon this humbled earth,
Although it is as common
As a child's birth.

For love as special as it is
Can really be a pain,
For those who seem to fall in love
Over and over again.

When love seems to not understand
This feels how it usually is
Picks out those who seem to be
Least interested in your biz.

Love seems to be the worst thing
To be caught within,
You can always feel the pain
As if left by a pin.

For those who cannot keep the love
That they thought they got,
They wish they couldn't remember
They wish they had forgot.

If you find your special person
And they are true to you,
Be forever thankful
And treat them as they treat you.

Visions

Dreams; What are they?
Are they wishes, hopes, or desires
Trying to be heard,
Or are they really something else?
Something totally different
Another's soul pressed into your head
Buy a higher being from another place
A God of sorts, the supernatural.
You may think what you will
You may feel as you like
Opinions on these visions
Are yours for all your life.

Needed

If a friend is ever lonely
They can give me a call
Friendship is a special gift
For which you go through it all.
Friends mean the world to us
Be forever in their debt,
Once you find that special friend
The best friend ever yet.
You worry that your friends will leave
When they find someone new,
You hope they know that you will be
A friend forever true.
Friends or family that you've chosen
You want them in your life,
Losing friends, you thought were true
Interrupts your whole life.
Be kind to other people
And I hope that they do the same,
Relationships go both ways
Don't make them a game.